Moving to Britain

U

PROJECTS

Falkirk Council

By Deborah Chancellor
Photography by Chris Fairclough

W
FRANKLIN WATTS
LONDON • SYDNEY

First published in 2008 by Franklin Watts

Franklin Watts,
338 Euston Road,
London, NW1 3BH

Franklin Watts Australia,
Level 17/207 Kent Street,
Sydney, NSW 2000

Series editor: Sarah Peutrill
Art director: Jonathan Hair
Design: Rita Storey
Photographs: Chris Fairclough (unless otherwise stated)

The Author and Publisher would like to thank the following for their help
in the preparation of this book: Volodymyr, Liuda and Katya and the staff
and pupils at Avondale Park Primary School, Kensington, London.

Picture credits: bluliq/Shutterstock: 10t. Family's personal photographs:
cover (inset), 8t, 9b and t. Maksym Gorpenyuk/Shutterstock: 11b.
PhotoSky4t.com/Shutterstock: 11t

Dewey number: 304.8'41'0477

ISBN: 978 0 7496 7861 6

Printed in China

Franklin Watts is a division of Hachette Children's Books,
an Hachette Livre UK company.
www.hachettelivre.co.uk

Contents

Words in **bold** are in the glossary on page 28.

All about me

My name is Katya. I am nine years old and I live in Kensington, West London. I like playing tennis and football, and I also enjoy swimming.

I have a tennis lesson after school on Fridays.

My school friends helped me learn English when I first arrived in Britain.

My family came to Britain from Ukraine three years ago. I speak three **languages**, Ukrainian, Russian and English. At home, I speak Ukrainian and Russian with my family, and I speak English at school.

Try talking in Ukrainian!

The Ukrainian alphabet is different to the English alphabet. It is called a cyrillic alphabet. There are 33 letters in the Ukrainian alphabet.

Hi	**Привіт** (pryvit)
My name is …	**Моє ім'я** … (moye im'ya)
How are you?	**Як справи?** (yak spravi)
Thank you	**Дякую** (d'yakuyu)
Bye bye	**Бувайте** (buvaite)

Meet my family

I live with my mum and dad. My dad is a **diplomat** at the Ukrainian **Embassy** in Britain.

When Dad got this job, we had to move from our home in Ukraine to come and live in Britain.

We live in an **apartment** near Dad's work. He walks to work every day.

I don't have any brothers or sisters, but I have five cousins who live in Ukraine. My grandparents also live in Ukraine, in the city of Kharkiv. I visit them when I go back to Ukraine in the summer holidays.

I miss my family in Ukraine, but I phone and send emails to keep in touch. Sometimes I write letters too.

9

About Ukraine

Ukraine is a country in Eastern Europe. It is roughly the same size as France. It takes about three hours to fly from London to Kiev, Ukraine's **capital city**.

Ukraine has **borders** with seven countries.

Ukraine

I like showing my friends where Ukraine is on a map.

Many Ukrainians go on holiday to Crimea, in southern Ukraine. Crimea is almost completely surrounded by the Black Sea.

Katya's mum says:

"In Ukraine, it is very hot in the summer, and freezing cold in the winter. I think Katya misses the deep winter snow – it doesn't snow that much in London!"

Huge, grassy fields cover much of Ukraine. The land is very **fertile**, and many crops are grown. There are beautiful mountains in the west and far south of the country. Many Ukrainians go on holiday to the Black Sea coast in the south.

The Carpathian mountains in western Ukraine are very beautiful in winter.

11

My life in Ukraine

I was born in the city of Kharkiv in northeast Ukraine. My family lived in an apartment in the city. The city is famous for its **universities**, and it is the second biggest city in Ukraine, after Kiev.

This is me with my grandfather when I was three months old.

I like looking at pictures of Ukraine, to remind me of my home country.

When I was five and a half years old, my family moved to Kiev, which is about 500 km from Kharkiv. We only stayed in Kiev for a few months, so I don't remember it very well. Then we moved to Britain.

Katya's mum says:

"Katya's first word was 'papa', which means 'Daddy' in both Russian and Ukrainian. I speak Russian and Katya's dad also speaks Ukrainian."

Moving to Britain

We moved to Kensington, which is in west London.

We travelled to Britain by plane. The day after my family arrived in Britain, it was my sixth birthday! I was nervous about coming to London, because I didn't know how to speak English. The only words I knew how to say were 'yes' and 'no'.

Katya's mum says:

"When we moved here, Katya found it hard at first. She wanted to play with other children, but she couldn't understand what they were saying to her."

I was sad to leave my friends and family behind in Ukraine, but my mum knew how to cheer me up. She told me we were moving to a city where I could see huge dinosaur skeletons in a museum. I am a big dinosaur fan.

I love seeing dinosaur fossils in museums. They are so much bigger than me.

When I moved to Britain, I brought my favourite toys with me. I like to play with my dinosaur models.

Living in London

London is a big, modern city, just like Kiev. London is very busy, and there is lots of noise and traffic. Sometimes I go shopping with my mum. I like going to Portobello Road market to buy fruit and vegetables.

Sometimes, we buy **ingredients** to make borsch. This is a kind of soup, made with beetroot and other vegetables.

My favourite park in Kensington is Holland Park. It takes ten minutes to walk there from our apartment.

Kensington has some lovely, quiet parks to play in. There is a playground in a park near my school, which I like to go to sometimes with my mum.

Katya's mum says:

"It didn't take Katya long to settle in London. It was easier for her than for me, because she was young when we moved, and didn't have strong memories of Ukraine."

Going to school

I was too young to go to school when I lived in Ukraine. Before my family came to Britain, I went to a **kindergarten** in Kiev for a few months. When we arrived in London, I started at a school in Kensington called Avondale Park Primary.

I joined Avondale Park School in Year 2. I am very happy here now, and have some good friends.

Sometimes Nana listens to me read in English. I am much better now than I used to be.

My first teachers at Avondale Park School were called Alan, Eve, Jackie and Maya. I was lucky, because Maya could speak to me in Russian! The **language support teacher** at my school is called Nana. She likes to see how my English has improved since I got here.

Alan, one of Katya's teachers says:

"I helped Katya learn English when she arrived. She made very quick progress, and settled easily, making friends right from the start."

My school day

I walk to school with my mum. It takes us about five minutes to get there. My school day always begins at 9am, and ends at 3.30pm. In Ukraine, schools usually start at 8.30am, and finish at different times each day, depending on the lessons you have.

Welcome to Avondale

There are about 400 children at my school. They come from many different countries, and speak lots of languages.

My favourite subject is art, but I also enjoy science, history and geography.

At school, my best friends are called Tia, Jasmine, Alfie and Josie. I used to have some Ukrainian school friends, but they moved back to Ukraine last summer.

Tia, Katya's friend, says:

"Katya is good at thinking up all kinds of new games to play. She is very kind to me, and she is my closest friend."

My free time

My parents have some friends in Kensington who speak Ukrainian and Russian. On Fridays, we all meet in the park, so the children can play football together. We speak in English, even though we can all speak Russian and Ukrainian. We are used to speaking English at school.

Alfie, Katya's friend, says:

"I like being with Katya because she has lots of energy. She is always jumping about!"

I like wearing my Ukrainian football shirt, and I am usually the goalie when we play football.

I also like to relax at home in our apartment. I enjoy reading books. Every night, I read three different books, in English, Ukrainian and Russian.

It is good to practise reading in different languages.

Keeping traditions

I like helping in the kitchen, especially at Christmas.

In Ukraine, we celebrate Christmas Day on January 7th. This is because we belong to the **Eastern Orthodox** Church, which has a different **calendar of festivals**. Now my family lives in Britain, we have two Christmas Days! We always have lots of fun at this time of year.

In Ukraine, Father Christmas is called 'Father Frost'. This is me with Father Frost and my parents at a Christmas party in London.

At Easter, we decorate eggs with pretty patterns. Ukrainian decorated eggs are called **pysanky eggs**. The **traditional** way to make pysanky eggs is to use wax and coloured dyes.

I paint my Easter eggs because it is easy to decorate them this way.

My future

Next summer, when my dad stops working at the embassy in London, my family will return to Ukraine. For the first time in my life, I will go to a Ukrainian school. I have started having Ukrainian lessons twice a week, to help me get better at this language.

I always work hard, so I do as well as I can.

When I grow up, I would like to be a teacher, like Mary, my Year 5 class teacher.

At the moment I don't want to leave Britain, because I have got used to it and I like it here. But there are lots of other places I might go to one day – perhaps Spain, France, Russia or the United States of America.

Glossary

apartment
A flat, or set of rooms, where people live.

border
A boundary between two different countries.

calendar of festivals
A list of special celebrations in the year.

capital city
The most important city in a country.

diplomat
Somebody who works for a country's government, to help keep good relations with other governments.

Eastern Orthodox
A branch of the Christian religion that is found mainly in Russia, Greece, Eastern Europe and the Middle East.

embassy
The office of a country's diplomats in the capital city of another country.

fertile
Land that is good for growing lots of crops.

ingredient
One of the things used in a recipe to cook food.

kindergarten
A nursery school for very young children.

language
The words used by a group of people to communicate with each other.

language support teacher
A teacher who helps children learn a language.

pysanky eggs
Ukrainian Easter eggs that are decorated in a traditional way, using special wax and coloured dyes.

traditional
A way of doing something that has not changed for a very long time.

university
A place where young people go to study after they have left school.

Ukraine fact file

• The distance between London and Kiev is 2,134km. Ukraine is two hours ahead of the UK, so when it is 12 noon in London, it is 2pm in Kiev.

• Around 46.3 million people live in Ukraine. Most Ukrainians speak Ukrainian and Russian, but the official language is Ukrainian. (Russian used to be the official language when Ukraine was part of the Soviet Union before 1991.)

• Some Ukrainians move to Britain to find work, and settle well into local communities here. Many work in the farming, food and service industries, and bring up their children in this country.

• Most Ukrainians follow the Eastern Orthodox Christian religion. There are also some Catholics, Protestants, Jews and Muslims in Ukraine.

• Football is a very popular sport in Ukraine. Andrij Shevchenko is one of Ukraine's most famous footballers.

• The Ukrainian currency is the Hryvnia. One Hryvnia is made up of 100 Kopeks.

• Children in Ukraine start primary school at six years old, after about three years in Kindergarten. They study for 11 years until they are 17.

• A typical school dinner in Ukraine has three courses and a fruit drink, for example traditional vegetable soup (borsch), followed by meat cutlet and mashed potato, then pancakes for dessert.

• In Ukraine, the school year starts on September 1st and ends on May 31st. There are four holidays: one week in November, two weeks for New Year, one week in March and three months in the summer.

Ukrainian flag

Index

Further information

www.ukraine.com
www.ucrainica.info
www.encyclopediaofukraine.com
These websites give general information about Ukraine.

http://Kharkiv.vbelous.net
This website gives information about Kharkiv, where Katya was born.

www.ukrainianegg.com
This website gives information about traditional Ukrainian pysanky eggs.

Note to parents and teachers: Please note that these websites are **not** specifically for children and we strongly advise that Internet access is supervised by a responsible adult.